Fierce Jobs
Stunt Performers

by Julie Murray

Dash!
LEVELED READERS
An Imprint of Abdo Zoom • abdobooks.com

2

2 Dash!
LEVELED READERS

Level 1 – Beginning
Short and simple sentences with familiar words or patterns for children who are beginning to understand how letters and sounds go together.

Level 2 – Emerging
Longer words and sentences with more complex language patterns for readers who are practicing common words and letter sounds.

Level 3 – Transitional
More developed language and vocabulary for readers who are becoming more independent.

THIS BOOK CONTAINS RECYCLED MATERIALS

abdobooks.com

Published by Abdo Zoom, a division of ABDO, PO Box 398166, Minneapolis, Minnesota 55439. Copyright © 2021 by Abdo Consulting Group, Inc. International copyrights reserved in all countries. No part of this book may be reproduced in any form without written permission from the publisher. Dash!™ is a trademark and logo of Abdo Zoom.

Printed in the United States of America, North Mankato, Minnesota.
052020
092020

Photo Credits: Alamy, AP Images, Getty Images, iStock, Shutterstock
Production Contributors: Kenny Abdo, Jennie Forsberg, Grace Hansen, John Hansen
Design Contributors: Dorothy Toth, Neil Klinepier, Laura Graphenteen

Library of Congress Control Number: 2019956151

Publisher's Cataloging in Publication Data

Names: Murray, Julie, author.
Title: Stunt performers / by Julie Murray
Description: Minneapolis, Minnesota : Abdo Zoom, 2021 | Series: Fierce jobs | Includes online resources and index.
Identifiers: ISBN 9781098221133 (lib. bdg.) | ISBN 9781644944080 (pbk.) |
    ISBN 9781098222116 (ebook) | ISBN 9781098222604 (Read-to-Me ebook)
Subjects: LCSH: Stunt performers--Juvenile literature. | Daredevils--Juvenile literature. | Motion picture industry--Juvenile literature. | Hazardous occupations--Juvenile literature. | Occupations--Juvenile literature.
Classification: DDC 791.43028--dc23

Table of Contents

Stunt Performers............4

Stunts and Tools
in Hollywood..............10

More Facts...............22

Glossary.................23

Index....................24

Online Resources..........24

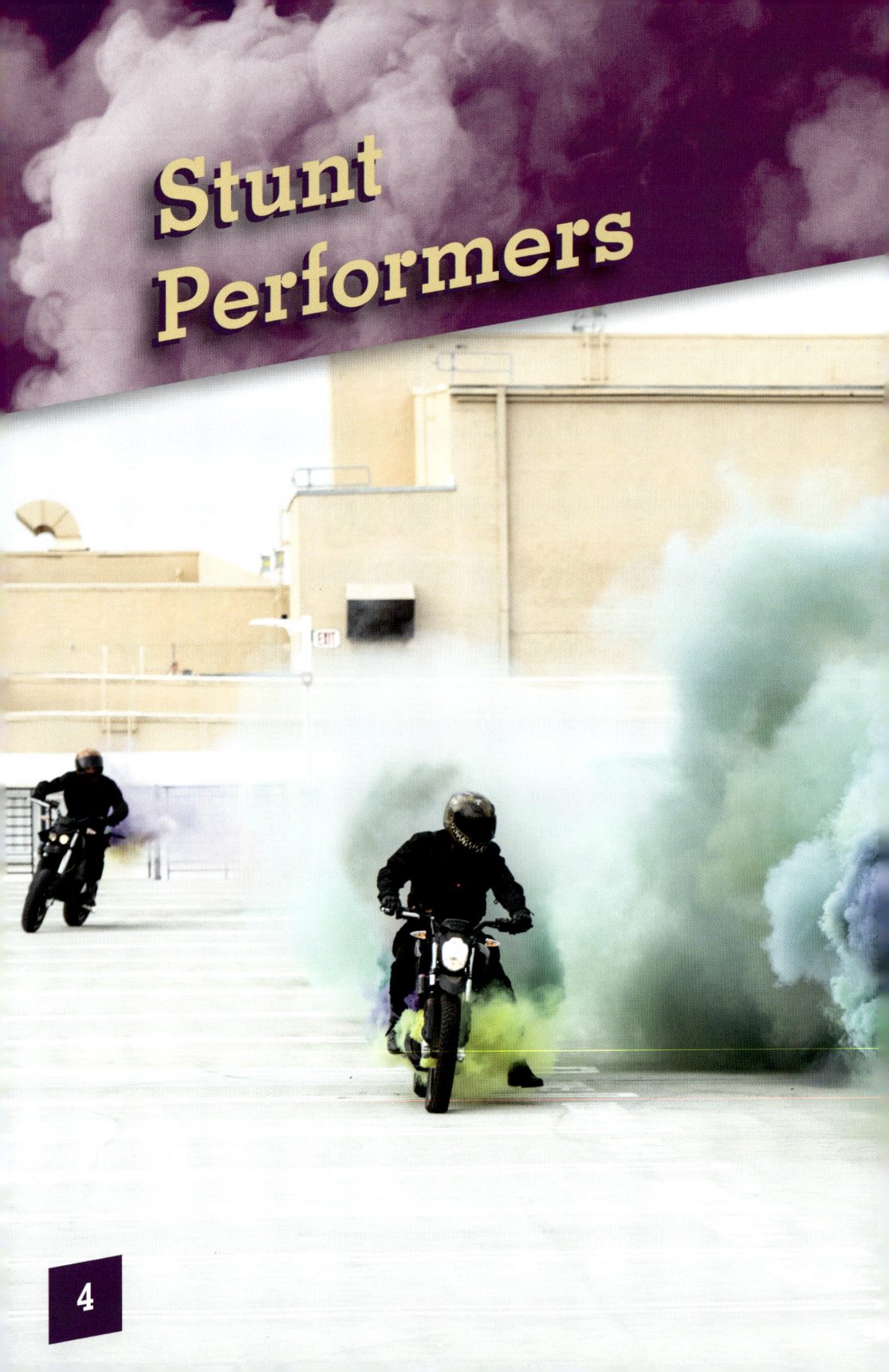

Stunt Performers

Stunt performers are **skilled** athletes. Some work on movie and TV **sets**. Others entertain crowds. Some do both!

Evel Knievel was a famous stunt performer and **daredevil**. He attempted more than 75 huge ramp-to-ramp motorcycle jumps!

7

Stunt performers in Hollywood do dangerous stunts in place of an actor. Most have to look like the actor to get the job. Some **specialize** in certain stunts.

9

Stunts and Tools in Hollywood

Falling is a big part of a stunt performer's job. Falls from high places can be dangerous. If performers land wrong, they can get hurt.

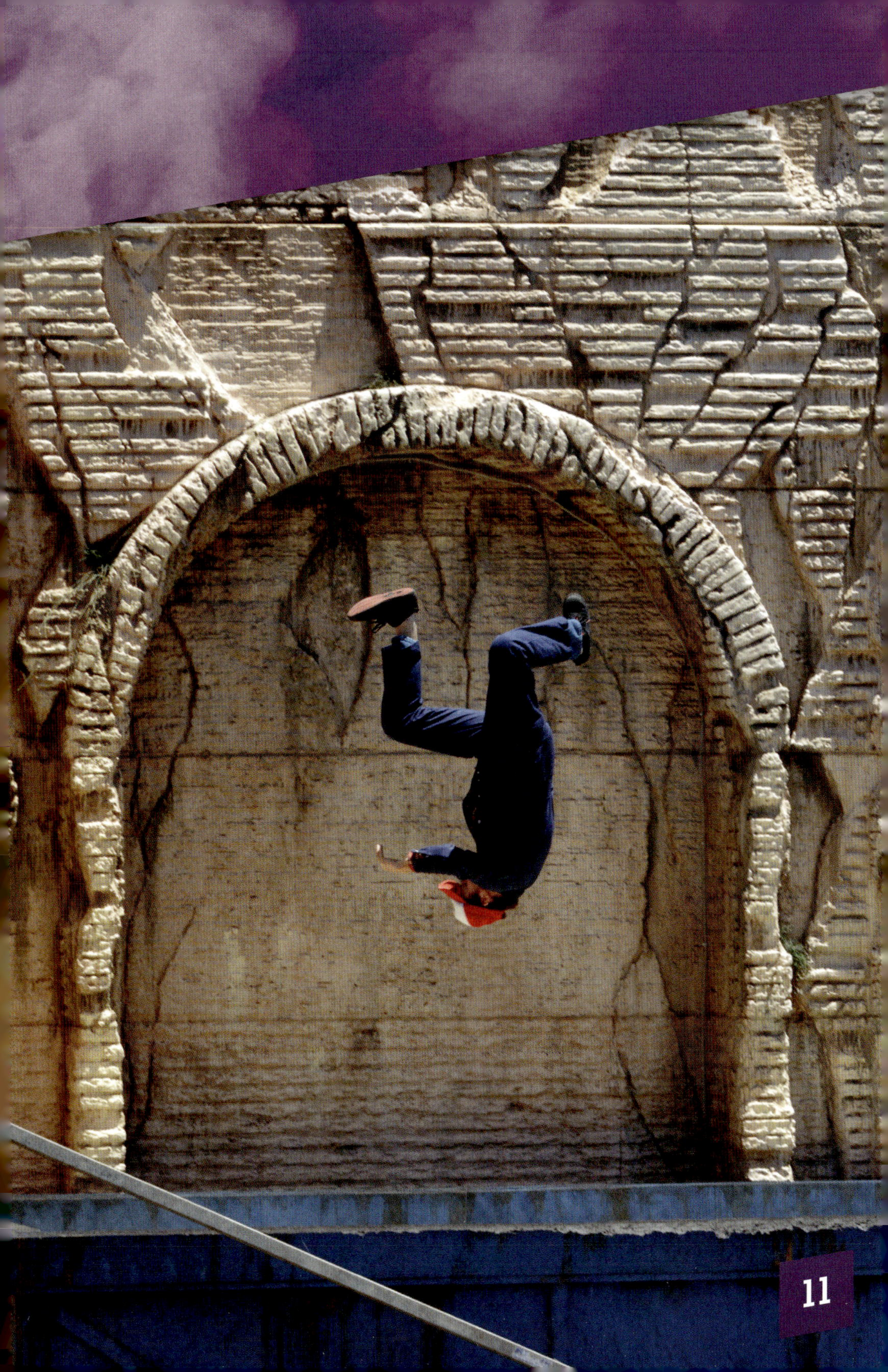

Stunt performers fall into water, foam pits, and boxes. This creates a soft landing. They sometimes wear a **harness** too.

13

Stunt performers often break through fake glass. They even jump between buildings and out of moving cars!

15

High-speed chases on film **sets** often end in crashes. Stunt performers must have perfect timing to avoid injury.

17

18

Fire stunts are also dangerous. Stunt performers wear fire-resistant suits. They cover their hair and skin with a special gel.

Stunt performers have a dangerous job to do. But with the right training, they can safely entertain people for years to come!

21

More Facts

- Many stunt performers train at stunt school. The International Stunt School in Seattle, Washington, is one of them.

- Stunt performers take on more than half of all movie-related injuries. Some have even died on movie **sets**.

- In movies, glass that breaks is often made of sugar. Other fake glass is made using plastic. These break easily and are less likely to cause injury to the stunt performer.

Glossary

daredevil – a person who puts himself or herself in danger by doing daring or dangerous stunts.

harness – a form of protective equipment designed to keep a person from falling or injuring themselves.

set – an artificial setting for a scene of a movie or television show.

skilled – having or showing the ability to perform a certain task well.

specialize – to concentrate on and become an expert in a particular subject or skill.

Index

cars 14, 16

fire 19

Hollywood 8, 14, 16

injury 10, 16

Knievel, Evil 6

motorcycle 6

movies 5, 8

safety 12, 16, 19, 20

stunt double 8

stunts 6, 8, 10, 12, 14, 19

TV 5, 8

Online Resources

Booklinks NONFICTION NETWORK
FREE! ONLINE NONFICTION RESOURCES

To learn more about stunt performers, please visit **abdobooklinks.com** or scan this QR code. These links are routinely monitored and updated to provide the most current information available.